Settlers, Soldiers, and Scalps

True Stories about
Settlers, Soldiers, Indians, and Outlaws
on the Pennsylvania Frontier

JOHN L. MOORE

Mechanicsburg, Pennsylvania   USA

Published by Sunbury Press, Inc.
50 West Main Street
Mechanicsburg, Pennsylvania 17055

www.sunburypress.com

Although the people whose experiences are chronicled in this book are dead, their stories survive in letters, diaries, journals, official reports, depositions, interrogations, examinations, minutes, and memoirs. These sources are quoted liberally. An occasional ellipsis indicates where words or phrases have been omitted. Punctuation and spelling have been modernized.

For information about special discounts for bulk purchases, please contact Sunbury Press Orders Dept. at (855) 338-8359 or orders@sunburypress.com.

To request one of our authors for speaking engagements or book signings, please contact Sunbury Press Publicity Dept. at publicity@sunburypress.com.

ISBN: 978-1-62006-516-7 (Trade Paperback)
Library of Congress Control Number: 2014956358

FIRST SUNBURY PRESS EDITION: November 2014

Product of the United States of America
0 1 1 2 3 5 8 13 21 34 55

Set in Bookman Old Style
Designed by Lawrence Knorr
Cover by Lawrence Knorr
Cover Art "Rifleman" by Andrew Knez, Jr.
Edited by Janice Rhayem

Continue the Enlightenment!

JOHN L. MOORE's

FRONTIER PENNSYLVANIA SERIES

Bows, Bullets, & Bears
Cannons, Cattle, & Campfires
Forts, Forests, & Flintlocks
Pioneers, Prisoners, & Peace Pipes
Rivers, Raiders, & Renegades
Settlers, Soldiers, & Scalps
Traders, Travelers, & Tomahawks
Warriors, Wampum, & Wolves

Author's Note on Quotations

I have taken a journalist's approach to writing about the people whose lives and experiences are chronicled in this book. Long dead, they nonetheless speak to us through the many letters, diaries, journals, official reports, depositions, interrogations, examinations, minutes, and memoirs that they left behind.

Whenever possible, I have presented the people I have written about in their own words. My intent is to allow the reader a sense of immediacy with historical figures who lived two or more centuries ago. To accomplish this, I have occasionally omitted phrases or sentences from quotations, and I have employed an ellipsis (...) to indicate where I have done so. In some instances, I have modernized punctuation; and in others, spelling has been modernized.

John L. Moore
Northumberland, Pa.
October 2014

Dedication

For my brother, Donald E. Moore,
1st Sergeant, U.S. Army, Infantry, Retired

Acknowledgments

My thanks to my wife, Jane E. Pritchard-Moore, for editing the manuscript. Thanks also to Robert B. Swift for many valuable suggestions.

Escape From the Indians

1759

By January 1756, Marie LeRoy and Barbara Leininger were beginning to look more like Native American girls than Europeans. Until October 16, 1755, the girls had lived about half a mile apart on neighboring farms in Central Pennsylvania, south of modern Mifflinburg. Then a Delaware war party raided the German and Swiss homesteads northwest of present-day Sunbury and Selinsgrove along the Mahonoy Creek, a stream now called Penns Creek.

The raiders killed thirteen white settlers, including Marie's father and Barbara's brother and father, and took twenty-eight prisoners, many of them children

Site of the Penn's Creek Massacre, west of Selinsgrove.

1

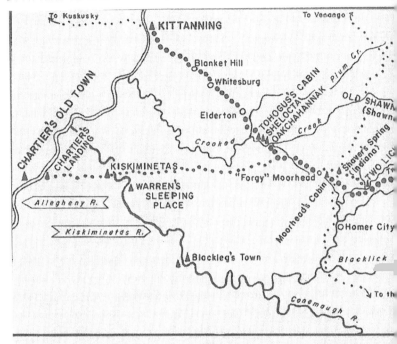

FRANKSTO

and women. The captives included Marie, Barbara, and Barbara's little sister, Regina.

Midwinter found Barbara and Marie, who were about fifteen, living in western Pennsylvania in the Delaware town of Kittanning, which occupied both the east and west banks of the Allegheny River. They wore dresses and moccasins made of deer skin and arranged their hair in the style of Indian girls. Their captors discouraged them from speaking German and required them to learn the Delaware language. The Delawares had brought the girls to Kittanning in December 1755 and used them as laborers. "We had to tan leather, to make shoes (moccasins), to clear land, to plant corn, to cut down trees and build huts, to wash and cook," they said afterwards. Sometimes

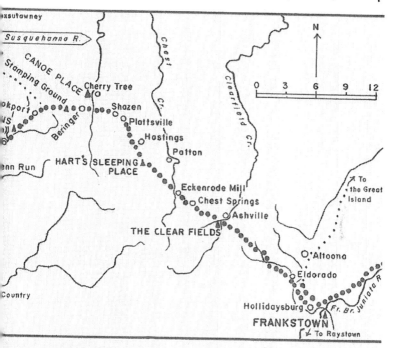

they had little to eat, and "we were forced to live on acorns, roots, grass and bark."

All winter and spring, as Delaware warriors made more and more raids into Pennsylvania, the number of white captives at Kittanning grew significantly. By summer, Marie and Barbara were among an estimated hundred white prisoners living in the town.

Located about fifty miles northeast of present-day Pittsburgh, where French soldiers had built Fort DuQuesne, Kittanning sat within a bend in the river. By the summer of 1756, the French and Indian War had been under way for a full year. Substantial numbers of Delawares who had lived in the Susquehanna River Valley had moved to the Allegheny to be beyond the reach of the soldiers who served in Pennsylvania's newly organized army. Many of these

3

Indians had settled in and around Kittanning, which had become an important community for the Delawares. These Indians had aligned themselves with the French, who supplied them with guns and ammunition, and encouraged them to send war parties to Pennsylvania and the other English colonies east of the Appalachian Mountains. The Allegheny River provided a natural link between Kittanning and Fort DuQuesne and other French posts along the Allegheny.

Excellent Location

The town also enjoyed an excellent defensive location. More than one hundred miles of forested mountains separated Kittanning from the nearest Pennsylvania forts. Less than a hundred warriors lived in the town, but they included two important war chiefs—Shingas the Terrible and Captain Jacobs, who liked to boast, "I can burn any fort made of wood." Indeed, in late July 1756 Captain Jacobs had taken, and torched, a stockade post called Fort Granville along the Juniata River near present-day Lewistown. In the fighting, the Indians had killed the officer in command at the post, Lieutenant Edward Armstrong.

The Indians to whom Marie LeRoy and Barbara Leininger belonged lived on the Allegheny's west bank, the section in which Shingas resided. As the townspeople—Indians, prisoners, and a small number of visiting French soldiers—settled down for the night of Tuesday, September 7, 1756, some 250 Pennsylvania soldiers, nearly all of them on foot, were quietly advancing from the southeast. Led by Lieutenant Colonel John Armstrong, the dead lieutenant's brother, the Pennsylvanians had made a ten-day march from the Juniata River Valley in order to attack Kittanning. The moonlight was bright enough for the soldiers to get quite close to the town's eastern section. Hardly suspecting an attack, the Delawares were having a nighttime festival. "We were guided by

Lieutenant Colonel John Armstrong

the beating of the drum, and the whooping of the warriors at their dance," Colonel Armstrong said later.

Marie and Barbara were likely asleep when, at daybreak, the soldiers moved into the town's eastern section and started shooting. The cabin of Captain Jacobs was in this area, and he "immediately gave the war whoop, and ... cried, 'White men were at last come, and they would have scalps enough,'"Armstrong said later.

The attack made a vivid impression on one participant, a Pennsylvania soldier named Robert Robison. "We rushed down to the town," Robison wrote

5

later. "The Indians' dogs barked, and (at) the first house we came to, the Indian came out and held his hand as if shading the light from his eyes, looking towards us until five guns fired at him. He then ran and with a loud voice called *Shewanick*," which was the Delaware word for white people. At this house, "a young woman, a prisoner, ... came out with both her hands raised up, but the guns firing so fast, she got frightened and ran back to the house again," Robison said. Fierce fighting quickly developed as the warriors defended the town.

On the West Shore

On the west shore the sound of gunfire coming from across the river awoke and terrified everyone, Indians and captives alike. Indian men grabbed their weapons and hurried across the river to help repel the invaders. The women gathered their children and prisoners, including Barbara and Marie, and led them rapidly into the woods on the western edge of the town. As the girls said later, "We were immediately conveyed 10 miles farther into the interior in order that we might have no chance of trying ... to escape."

On the east shore the fighting lasted until midday. The Pennsylvanians couldn't manage to surround Kittanning, but did set fire to nearly thirty cabins. When Armstrong ordered his men to burn the town, a soldier named John Ferguson, reacting sharply, "swore by the Lord God that he would," Robison said. "He goes to a house covered with bark and takes a slice of bark which had fire on it. He rushes up to the cover of (Captain) Jacobs' house and held it there until it had burned about one yard square. Then he ran, and the Indians fired at him. The smoke blew about his legs, but the shot missed."

As Armstrong's soldiers moved among the cabins to torch them, they called on the Indians inside to surrender, "but one of the Indians in particular answered, and said he was a man, and would not be a prisoner; upon which he was told in Indian he would

6

be burnt. To this answer, he didn't care, for he would kill four or five before he died," Armstrong said.

At one house, the fire got so hot that two men and a woman jumped out and started to run toward a nearby cornfield. All three "were immediately shot down by our people surrounding the houses," the colonel said. "It was thought Captain Jacob tumbled himself out at a garret ... window, at which he was shot—our prisoners offering to be qualified to the powder horn and pouch there taken off him, which they say he had lately got from a French officer in exchange for Lieutenant Armstrong's boots, which he carried from Fort Granville, where the lieutenant was killed." Captain Jacobs had kept kegs of gunpowder in his cabin. The powder kegs caught fire and exploded. The blast blew the roof off.

With much of Kittanning's eastern section in ruins, the Pennsylvanians withdrew nearly as quickly as they had come. They had managed to liberate less than a dozen of the white prisoners. Barbara Leininger and Marie Leroy weren't among them.

In the days following the battle, when it became clear that the Pennsylvanians weren't coming back, the Indians returned to Kittanning, which Marie and Barbara described as "burned to the ground." One day the Indians decided to punish a prisoner, an English woman who had tried to run off with the Pennsylvania soldiers. She had actually escaped, but Indians who pursued Armstrong's column recaptured her and brought her back to Kittanning. "They scalped her," Barbara and Marie said. "Next, they laid burning splinters of wood here and there upon her body, and then they cut off her ears and fingers, forcing them into her mouth so that she had to swallow them." The woman's torture lasted most of the day, until around sunset when a French officer finished her off. The Indians "let her lie until the dogs came and devoured her."

Three Days Later

Three days after this event some Indians came in with another prisoner, an Englishman who had also attempted to escape. Marie and Barbara told how the Delawares burned him alive. "His screams were frightful to listen to," they said. The weather was stormy, and it rained so hard that the fire went out. The Indians fired gunpowder into his body. "When the poor man called for a drink of water, they brought ... melted lead and poured it down his throat." The molten metal quickly killed him.

Once Colonel Armstrong's Pennsylvanians had withdrawn to the east of the Allegheny Mountains, the English colonies didn't have a significant military presence within 150 miles of the French-held Ohio. Even so, during the weeks and months following the Kittanning raid, many Delawares moved farther west, deeper into Indian country and farther away from Pennsylvania and its army. Marie LeRoy and Barbara Leininger, together with many other prisoners, accompanied them. At first, the Indian named Galasko, who had become the girls' master or owner, took Marie and Barbara down the Allegheny to Fort DuQuesne, where he hired them out to soldiers in the garrison. "We worked for the French, and our Indian master drew our wages," they reported later. "In this place, thank God, we could again eat bread. Half a pound was given us daily. We might have had bacon, too, but we took none of it, for it was not good." The girls realized that their situation at the fort was only temporary. They also saw that the French soldiers liked them. "They tried hard to induce us to forsake the Indians and stay with them, making us various favorable offers," they said.

But after two months Galasko took the girls away from Fort DuQuesne and moved them to an Indian town along the Ohio River called Sawkunk, a settlement of Delawares, Shawnee, and Iroquois near the mouth of the Beaver River. When spring came in 1757, they moved again, this time to Kuskuski, a

Delaware town higher up the Beaver watershed at present-day New Castle. "We remained at this place for about one year and a half," the girls said. They grew corn and were given "hard work of every kind."

Surprise Visitor

In August 1758 they were surprised—and delighted—to find a German "who was not a captive, but free" in the town. He was Christian Frederick Post, a Moravian missionary sent west by the Pennsylvania colony as an envoy to encourage the Delawares to make peace. "We and all the other prisoners heartily wished him success ... We were, however, not allowed to speak with him. ... He himself, by the reserve with which he treated us, let us see that this was not the time to talk over our afflictions." The missionary's situation was hardly an enviable one. The Delawares had warned the captives not to attempt to engage him in conversation and predicted that Post would never manage to return to Pennsylvania safely. "We were greatly alarmed on his account," Barbara and Marie said, "for the French told us that, if they caught him, they would roast him alive for five days."

Post had crossed the Allegheny Mountains and come west on a peace mission with an important Delaware war chief, Pisquetomen. At Kuskuski, he met with Pisquetomen's brothers, Tamaqua and Shingas, in Shingas's cabin. The Indian leaders wanted to know, "Why don't you (the English) and the French fight in the old country and on the sea? Why do you come to fight in our country? This makes everybody believe that you only want to take and settle the land." The Moravian denied this. The English, Post said, wanted to drive the French away from the Ohio River Valley, not occupy the Indians' land. In the end, the Delawares signaled a willingness to enter into peace talks with the English. Their mission completed, Post and Pisquetomen left the Ohio territory in early September and headed east to inform colonial officials in Pennsylvania of their talks with the Delawares. The

9

girls from Mahonoy (Penns) Creek remained captives, as did scores if not hundreds of other white people living along the Ohio and its tributaries

As autumn came on, the Indians became increasingly concerned about an English army that was advancing on Fort DuQuesne from Pennsylvania. In early fall, news swept the Ohio villages that English soldiers had defeated a force of Indians and French some fifty miles east of Fort DuQuesne at a place called Loyal-Hannon (present-day Ligonier). The Indians living along the Allegheny and Ohio reacted by moving farther west—to the Muskingum River Valley about 150 miles away. "Before leaving," Barbara and Marie said later, "they destroyed their crops, and burned everything which they could not carry with them. We had to go along ..."

In late 1758, with a British army rapidly approaching from the east, the French withdrew from Fort DuQuesne, which they destroyed as they evacuated. The last soldiers to leave set fire to the wooden buildings and exploded gun powder stored in the magazines. The ruins were still smoldering when the English arrived the next day. The British immediately began to construct a new fort, rushing to finish it by the time winter set in. The outpost, which they named Fort Pitt, became one of the westernmost English forts in North America.

Winter of 1758-59

As the winter of 1758-59 progressed, word spread throughout the Native American towns along the Ohio and Muskingum Rivers that the British at Fort Pitt were welcoming Indians who came to trade. Indians who had been allied with the French soon arrived to make peace with the British and to trade. In greeting one of the first groups to arrive at the new fort, Colonel Henry Bouquet welcomed them and encouraged their hunters and trappers to bring their furs to the new post to trade. The outpost, which lay west of the Allegheny Mountains, proved difficult for the English to supply, and Colonel Hugh Mercer, whom Bouquet placed in command, often found it challenging to meet Indian expectations.

Even supplying the fort with the basics in provisions proved something of a challenge. Much if not most of the garrison's food supply had to be shipped over the mountains on horseback from British posts in the east. For instance, the commander at Fort Bedford, a British post one hundred miles to the east for Fort Pitt, in early February reported that he had sent ample stores of flour, pork, and beef, presumably transported over the Alleghenies by pack trains of horses. "I am satisfied they have three months provisions of these species, besides plenty of liquors, butter, tobacco, etc.," said the commander, Lieutenant Lewis Ourry of the Royal American Regiment.

The wares that attracted the Indians to Fort Pitt also had to be shipped in from the east. For instance, a train of thirty-nine horses loaded with trade goods for the Indians and destined for Fort Pitt left Fort Bedford on February 24, 1759. According to the commander at Bedford, the merchandise included more than 400 blankets; 11 yards of blue fabric for use in making breech clouts; nearly 200 coats in the French style, of which were 116 were brown and 80 were white; 20 shirts, of which 18 were checked and 2 were white, with ruffles; nearly 900 clasp knives; more than 300 scalping knives; 2,000 flints for flintlock rifles and pistols; 96 tomahawks; 20 guns; 2 pistols; 360 brass rings; and 72 jews harps. Notably absent: rum and other alcoholic beverages; the British military had strictly prohibited traders to provide liquor to Indians who came to the fort.

Colonel Dissatisfied

Colonel Mercer wasn't satisfied with the goods that Ourry had shipped from Fort Bedford and felt obligated to supplement these wares by purchasing trade goods from private merchants who had ventured to Pittsburgh. In a letter to Bouquet, he justified this by emphasizing his need to please Indians who came to Fort Pitt to trade. "They have brought a great many skins and fur and would return (home) extremely disgusted were they not taken off their hands ... About 60 Indians of different tribes are now here."

The French continued to come into the region to trade with the Indians. Although the French had abandoned Fort DuQuesne, they retained control of Fort Machault on the Allegheny River, a small post several days voyage above Fort DuQuesne at present-day Franklin. They also controlled the Great Lakes and occasionally traveled into the interior to trade. On March 6, for instance, Mercer reported that an Indian had told him that "an officer and 20 (French) men are at White Woman," a Delaware town at modern Warsaw, Ohio. "They have traded with the Indians for fur."

It was against this backdrop that Barbara Leininger, growing increasingly desperate, began hatching a plan to run away from the Indians and to return to Pennsylvania.

During the winter Barbara had befriended a young English captive, David Breckenridge, and the two had begun planning an escape. When Barbara told Marie about the plan, Marie said she wanted to go along. Marie and Barbara don't mention in their narrative that Marie had a strong motive for leaving the Delaware towns as quickly as she could, but a third prisoner, a young man named Hugh Gibson, reported that the Indians had decided that Marie—whom he refers to by her Indian name, "Pum-e-ra-moo"—would marry a Delaware man, "who had been selected for her."

A youth of eighteen, Gibson had become friendly with Marie, who expressed her displeasure at the prospect of marrying the man. "She told Gibson that she would sooner be shot than have him (the Delaware) for her husband, and she entreated him (Gibson), as did Barbara likewise, to unite with them in the attempt to run away." Gibson readily agreed.

Invited Friend

The girls' decision to invite Gibson was a good one. The youth had been taken prisoner near Robinson's Fort along Shermans Creek near present-day Loysville in Perry County in July 1756 while helping his mother look for their cows. Years later, Gibson recalled that the Indians had treated him harshly during his first months as a prisoner. "Many times they beat me most severely," he said. At one point, they even threatened to kill him "and ... they sent me to gather wood to burn myself, but I cannot tell whether they intended to do it or to frighten me."

Within a few months, Gibson's captor took him to Kittanning. In the days following Armstrong's attack on the town, he was among the white prisoners forced to watch the execution of some of the captives who had attempted to run off with the Pennsylvania soldiers. In carrying out the execution of a woman, the Indians stripped her, "bound her to a post," and applied "hot irons to her whilst the skin stuck to the iron at every touch," he said later. Gibson recognized one of the men torturing her as a warrior from the Shermans Creek raid. Gibson noted that his mother's scalp "hung as a trophy from his belt."

Gibson had been adopted into a prominent family of Delawares. Shingas was one of his adopted brothers. Another was Pisquetomen, or, as Gibson referred to him, Bisquittam. During the ceremony in which Bisquittam adopted him, the Indian addressed him and said, "I am your brother." Bisquittam matter-of-factly introduced the boy to other members of his new family. "This is your brother," he said. "That is your brother. This is your cousin, that is your cousin, and all these are your friends." Gibson learned that the family was adopting him to replace one of Bisquittam's six brothers, who had been killed by Cherokee Indians allied with the English. As Gibson recalled the episode years later, Bisquittam "then painted his adopted brother and told him that the Indians would take him to the river, wash away all his white blood and make him an Indian." Gibson's new relatives then escorted him to the Allegheny, "plunged him into the water, thoroughly washed him from head to foot and conducted him back to his master and brother." They then dressed him, Indian-style, in a "breech-cloth, leggins, capo (cap), porcupine moccasins, and a shirt."

During the years that followed, Gibson's Delaware relatives taught him Indian-style hunting techniques and other forest skills. By the winter of 1758-59, he had become a knowledgeable woodsman.

Time to Escape

In late February most of the Indian men at Muskingum set out for Fort Pitt to sell the pelts they had accumulated during the hunting season. With the men gone, the four teenagers—Marie LeRoy, Barbara Leininger, Hugh Gibson, and David Brackenridge—realized that a moment of opportunity had arrived. Their resolve to escape strengthened. Meanwhile, as Barbara and Marie wrote later, the Indian women "traveled ten miles up the country to gather roots, and we accompanied them. Two men went along as a guard."

The girls thought that the situation might provide a chance to escape. They and the boys picked a date, March 16, and formed a plan. Barbara pretended to be sick, and the Indian women let her put up a small hut, probably fashioned of tree branches covered with bark, for herself.

Events that occurred on March 14, 1759, proved to be crucial. As the day approached for the teenagers to make their escape, Gibson convinced his master to let him go hunting for deer for three days. "Bisquittam furnished him with a gun, a powder-horn well filled, 13 bullets, a deer skin for making moccasins and sinews to sew them, two blanket and two shirts." But Gibson had lied to Bisquittam. He took the supplies that the Indian had given him—as well as a tomahawk and a flint and steel for making fire—and promptly headed for a late night rendezvous with Marie LeRoy, Barbara Leininger, and David Brackenridge at a predetermined spot.

Also on March 14, the women sent Marie back to Muskingum to fetch two dogs they had left behind in the village. The same day, Barbara emerged from her hut long enough to visit another captive, a German woman named Mary. Indian raiders had kidnapped Mary, the wife of a miller, from a settlement along the South Branch of the Potomac River.

Too Lame to Go

Mary had been helping Marie and Barbara plan the escape, and she had intended to go along. In preparation, she had secretly put aside a small quantity of foods and some pelts, but Barbara discovered that Mary "had ... become lame and could not think of going along."

When Barbara informed her that the absence of the men had created an ideal time for an escape, Mary insisted that Barbara take her secret stash of goods: "two pounds of dried meat, a quart of corn and four pounds of sugar." Mary also gave her some skins that Barbara and Marie could use if they needed to make new moccasins along the way.

"On the 16th of March, in the evening, Gibson reached Barbara Leininger's hut, and at 10 o'clock, our whole party, consisting of us two girls, Gibson and David Breckenridge, left Muskingum. This town lies on a river ... We had to pass many huts inhabited by the savages, and knew that there were at least 16 dogs with them. ... Not a single one of these dogs barked. Their barking would at once have betrayed us."

The runaways soon reached the Muskingum River, and Barbara recited a prayer that she had learned as a youngster. One line, translated from the German, said plainly: "O bring us safely across this river."

Within minutes, they found a raft that an Indian had left along the riverbank. "Thanking God ... we got on board and pushed off." The current proved stronger than they had anticipated, and "we were carried almost a mile down the river before we could reach the other side." Finally across the Muskingum, the escapees struck out in a direction they hoped would lead to Pennsylvania. "Full of anxiety and fear, we fairly ran that whole night and all next day (March 17), when we lay down to rest without venturing to kindle a fire."

Years later, Gibson, in telling about the night they ventured onto the Muskingum, provided a few additional details. "It was about the full moon," he said. "The Muskingum was very high, and there were two rafts near the women's fire. They unmoored one, and it soon went down the river. They entered the other with their accoutrements, the women taking their kettle, crossed the Muskingum and let the raft go adrift. They traveled with all possible expedition during the residue of the night in a southerly direction in order to deceive the Indians, in case they should attempt to follow them. In the morning they steered a due east course."

Adventure-Filled Day

March 18 provided another full day of adventure. As the runaways hurried through the forest, Gibson spotted a bear among some large rocks. He quickly raised his gun and fired. As Marie and Barbara said later, "The animal fell, but when he (Gibson) ran with his tomahawks to kill it, it jumped up and bit him in the feet, leaving three wounds. We all hastened to his assistance." The bear "escaped into some narrow holes among the rocks, where we could not follow."

Injured but undaunted, Gibson joined the others as they continued their trek. The injuries "pained me very much," he said later, "and retarded my journey ..." The girls, incidentally, referred to Gibson as Owen rather than Hugh. Later in the day, despite his wounds, "Owen Gibson shot a deer. We cut off the hind-quarters and roasted them at night," Barbara and Marie said later. Years later, in describing this incident, Gibson recalled that the runaways had skinned the buck, then used the skin to form "a kind of hopper" for carrying the venison.

Gibson shot another deer during the morning of March 19, and the animal "furnished us with food for that day. In the evening, we got to the Ohio (River) at last, having made a circuit of over a hundred miles in order to reach it." Barbara and Marie didn't list any landmarks, but they had possibly reached the Ohio at a point between the modern Ohio city of Marietta, where the Muskingum joins the Ohio and Wheeling, West Virginia. Gibson in his memoir reported they had "reached the Ohio River above Wheeling."

Indian travelers frequently peeled the bark off trees and used the exposed wood as a kind of message board. Using black or red paint, they drew symbols and pictographs to leave information for subsequent passersby. The girls and their companions had learned to read these messages. "From the signs which the Indians had put up, we saw that we were about 150 miles from Fort DuQuesne," they said.

The travelers decided to cross the Ohio and walk "straight toward the rising of the sun." They spent the evening on the river's Ohio side, and at "about midnight, the two Englishmen rose and began to work at a raft, which was finished by morning. We got on board and safely crossed the river." Gibson recalled that he collected poles to fashion the raft "and bound it together with (strips of) elm bark and grapevines." Using tomahawks as their principal tools, they fashioned a raft that was sufficiently sturdy to carry them across the Ohio, "but in crossing ... I lost my gun," Gibson said. They crossed at night, reached the river's eastern shore, and entered a deep ravine. "Here they kindled a fire, cooked and ate their meat and spent the night," he said.

Sunrise

On the morning of March 20 they started walking toward the sunrise, and seven days later came to Little

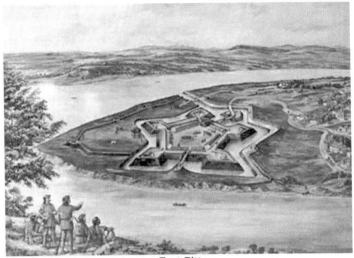

Fort Pitt

Beaver Creek, just east of the present-day Ohio-Pennsylvania border. They were now less than fifty miles from Fort Pitt. As they continued, the travelers encountered a variety of misfortunes. To begin with, the weather during the last week of March became cold and wet. To make matters worse, their provisions were running low. At one point, Barbara fell into the water and nearly drowned. Another day, Owen Gibson lost the flint and steel that he used to make fire. "Hence, we had to spend four nights without fire amidst rain and snow," the girls said.

It was March 31 when the weary travelers reached Chartier's Creek, a stream that emptied into the Ohio several miles below Fort Pitt at modern McKees Rocks. They made a raft, but when all four attempted to cross the creek at once, "it threatened to sink, and Marie LeRoy fell off." The others rescued Marie, who narrowly escaped drowning. In the end, "we had to put back and let one of our men convey one of us across at a time," Barbara and Marie said later.

The fugitives pressed on. It was late afternoon by the time they reached the confluence of the Allegheny and Monongahela Rivers, where the Ohio was formed. They were on the southern shore of the Monongahela, directly opposite the English fort. They stood on the riverbank and called for help. Soldiers in Fort Pitt heard their shouts, and presently, the commandant sent a rowboat over to them. The soldiers became wary as they approached the shore. "They thought we were Indians," Marie and Barbara said later. That was understandable. All four were dressed in deerskin clothing and moccasins and wore their hair in Indian style. It was beginning to get dark, and the soldiers "wanted us to spend the night where we were, saying they would fetch us in the morning."

The runaways retorted "that we were English prisoners who had escaped from the Indians and that we were wet and cold and hungry," the girls said.

The soldiers wanted to know how many people wanted to cross. The runaways insisted there were only four of them, but the soldiers, suspicious and wary of treachery, demanded details and names. David Breckenridge, Gibson recalled, "told them that he was taken at Loyal Hanna, where he drove a wagon numbered 39." Some of the soldiers knew that this statement was correct. Gibson said that he "informed them that he was taken near Robinson's fort and that Israel Gibson was his brother. Some present were acquainted with the latter." In turn, the girls said that Indians had taken them during a raid along the Mahonoy, an old name for Penns Creek.

In the End

In the end, the soldiers relented and transported them across the Monongahela to Fort Pitt. According to Marie and Barbara's version of events, the soldiers came in one boat, but Hugh Gibson's account stated that there were "two boats with 15 men well-armed."

Gibson gave more details than the girls did. The soldiers' orders, he said, "were, in case there should appear to be more than four, to fire upon them." As they approached the western shore, "the boatmen directed the captives to stand back upon the rising ground and to come forward one at a time as they should be called," Gibson said.

The fugitives did as directed, and were soon traveling across the river. According to Barbara and Marie, "There was an Indian with the soldiers in the boat. He asked us if we could speak good Indian." Marie said that she could, and the man, speaking in his native tongue, asked why she had run away. "She replied that her Indian mother had been so cross and had scolded her so constantly that she could not stay with her any longer." The girls could see that Marie's answer displeased the Indian, but the man replied diplomatically that "he was very glad we had safely reached the fort."

Nightfall

Night was falling by the time the boat reached the landing at Fort Pitt. "Most heartily did we thank God in Heaven for all the mercy which He showed us," the girls said. They felt especially grateful that they hadn't encountered any enemy Indians during their two-week escapade and that they had arrived safely at Pittsburgh. Marie and Barbara remembered all too well the months they had spent at the confluence during late autumn in 1756 while the French controlled it.

The British had erected Fort Pitt in the weeks after the French abandoned Fort DuQuesne in November 1758. The English commander was Colonel Hugh Mercer, and he readily welcomed the four newcomers. "Colonel Mercer helped and aided us in every way which lay in his power," Barbara and Marie said. "Whatever was on hand and calculated to refresh us was offered in the most friendly manner." Seeing that they had arrived dressed as Indians, "the colonel ordered for each of us a new chemise, a petticoat, a pair of stockings, garters and a knife." Shedding the clothing of their captivity and putting on European garments provided another proof of the change in their situation. Only now did they become truly confident

Colonel Hugh Mercer

that they had made good their escape from the Indians.

Colonel Mercer let the youngsters rest for a day and arranged for soldiers to escort them to Fort Ligonier, a stockade post about fifty miles to the east, on April 2. The officer who commanded the detachment was Lieutenant Samuel Miles. When they reached Fort Ligonier, Miles "presented each one of us with a blanket."

The youngsters remained at Fort Ligonier until mid-April, when on April 15 a small force led by Captain Weiser and Lieutenant Samuel J. Atlee took them to Fort Bedford, another fifty miles to the east. Rough and rutted, the dirt road that led east from Fort Ligonier crossed steep and rugged mountains to reach

Fort Bedford. English soldiers had constructed the road the previous summer as part of the British advance on Fort DuQuesne. Intended mainly for regiments of foot soldiers and convoys of wagons carrying military supplies, it cut through the forests in as straight a line as the army engineers had managed.

The ride from Fort Ligonier to Fort Bedford took another two days. The youngsters and the soldiers escorting them camped along the road the night of April 15. The next day offered a hard day's travel to Fort Bedford, "where we arrived in the evening of the 16th and remained a week." The stockade post stood along a branch of the Juniata River.

It was late April when a wagon convoy left Fort Bedford bound for Harris's Ferry (present-day Harrisburg). Owen Gibson remained at Fort Bedford, but Marie, Barbara, and David Breckenridge traveled the hundred-plus miles to Harrisburg in a wagon. All three carried passports that Lieutenant Henry Geiger had provided.

From Harris's Ferry, the three walked to Lancaster, which was about forty miles away. David Breckenridge stayed at Lancaster, and Barbara and Marie walked to Philadelphia. "We two girls arrived in Philadelphia on Sunday, the 6th of May."

Enterprising Publisher

An enterprising Philadelphia publisher soon persuaded the young women to write a narrative of their adventures and misfortunes as Indian captives. Written in German, it began with the October 16, 1755, attack on the Penns Creek settlements and ended with their arrival in Philadelphia more than three and a half years later.

The girls included a remarkable postscript to their narrative: a listing of nearly forty other white captives living with the Indians. These were "prisoners whom we met at the various places where we were during our captivity." They included Mary and James Lory, a brother and sister who were captured when the

THE SITUATION, HARBOUR &c. of THE CITY and PORT of PHILADELPHIA.

Pennsylvania soldiers surrendered Fort Granville, a colonial post on the Juniata River at present-day Lewistown, to the Indians and French in July 1756. Barbara and Marie thought that Mary was about fourteen and James twelve or thirteen. They had also encountered "Mary Taylor, an English woman captured at Fort Granville, together with a girl named Margaret."

Other captives included "an old Englishman, or Irishman, whose surname we do not know but whose Christian name is Dan, a cooper, captured on the Susquehanna." They had met Dan at the Indian town called Kaschkaschkung. At this place they had also seen "Anna Brielinger, wife of a German smith from Shamokin." By Shamokin, they referred to a sizable region along the Susquehanna River roughly centered around modern Sunbury. Anna and her husband, Jacob, had settled on the Penns Creek about two miles below present-day New Berlin.

The list of captives could have been much longer, because "we became acquainted with many other captives—men, women and children—in various Indian towns, but do not know or cannot remember their names."

One name that is notably absent from the litany is that of Barbara's younger sister, Regina Leininger.

Regina had been about twelve when the Delawares had raided Penns Creek. The sisters had been separated in the early days of their captivity.

During the 1870s, a bishop of the Moravian Church, Edmund de Schweinitz of Bethlehem, Pa., translated the "Narrative of Marie LeRoy and Barbara Leininger" into English. He did so at the request of John B. Linn and William H. Egle, who were gathering and compiling documents from Pennsylvania's colonial era for publication in a multi-volume collection called *Pennsylvania Archives, Second Series*. Linn and Egle included the girls' story in Volume VII, which the Commonwealth of Pennsylvania published in 1878.

Sections of this article dealing with Barbara Leininger and Marie LeRoy are based largely on Bishop de Schweinitz's translation of their 1759 narrative.

Indians Took Scalps as Trophies

April 1757

With hostile Indians lurking about the neighborhood, even a task as simple and routine as fetching firewood became incredibly dangerous for whites who had settled along the Pennsylvania frontier. Consider the case of Andreas Gundryman, a seventeen-year-old boy who lived with his family literally under the guns of Fort Hamilton, a small post protected by a small, log stockade in what is now Stroudsburg. The fort was situated in a corn field near the Gundryman farm house. To be specific, the house was about fifty-five yards from Fort Hamilton, which had been built in late 1755 and early 1756, during the French and Indian War. A small detachment of Pennsylvania soldiers was posted at the fort, and the

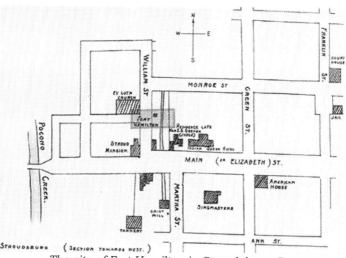

The site of Fort Hamilton in Stroudsburg, Pa.

Gundrymans and other families who lived in the immediate neighborhood felt a sense of security as spring arrived without any signs of Indian war parties.

Late in the afternoon of Wednesday, April 20, 1757, Andreas hitched a two-horse team to his father's sleigh and set out "to fetch some firewood" about a quarter of a mile from the fort. As a neighbor, John Williamson, reported two days later, it was nearly sunset when Williamson and several others heard two gunshots. Reacting immediately, Andreas's father, Henry Gundryman, and a colonial soldier, Conrad Freidenberg, started running up a hill toward the spot where the boy had gone for wood. Several members of the garrison heard the youngster shouting for help, then saw him running down the hill toward the fort, but efforts to rescue the boy failed. According to Williamson, "About 300 yards from this fort, they (the elder Gundryman and Freidenberg) found ... Andreas Gundryman lying dead and scalped quite to the eyes."

Settlers, Soldiers

The settlers and the soldiers quickly determined that the Indians who shot at the boy had missed. "As soon as they fired, Andreas ran, and they pursued him with their tomahawks and murdered him very barbarously," Williamson declared in a deposition he gave at Easton two days later. In making the deposition, Williamson told William Parsons, the justice of the peace, that he himself "saw two Indians run up the hill ... and as they went off set up the Indian war halloo. ..."

In taking the youth's hair, the warriors were following an ancient tradition. As Europeans began to colonize the Eastern Seaboard during the 1600s, they learned that native warriors often cut off—and kept as trophies—part of the scalp and hair of people that they had killed or wounded in warfare. This practice came to be known as scalping, and Europeans whose settlements were subject to Indian raids dreaded it. To be sure, the practice of scalping remained prevalent

26

during the eighteenth century, notably during both the French and Indian War and the American Revolution, but records and accounts of the prior century clearly show that scalping predated these conflicts.

For instance, most Native Americans who encountered colonists in New Sweden, a settlement that flourished briefly along the Delaware River during the mid-1600s, were friendly, but occasionally they killed Swedish settlers and harvested their hair, according to Israel Acrelius, a Swedish historian who lived in the Delaware Valley a century later.

New Sweden had been established in 1638, and Acrelius reported that Indians whom "the Swedes called Flatheads, for their heads were flat on the crown," sometimes visited in company with peaceful parties of Minnisink Indians from the Upper Delaware River. The Flatheads "were dangerous and murdered people when they found them alone in the woods. They first struck the person on the head so that he either died or swooned, after which they took off the skin of the head. ... That is called scalping ... and the skin of the head is called a scalp."

"An old Swedish woman ... had the misfortune to be scalped in this manner, yet lived many years thereafter and became the mother of a number of children. No hair grew on her head again, except what was short and fine," Acrelius said in his 1759 book, *A History of New Sweden*.

Two Soldiers

Two soldiers who took part in eighteenth century wars in North America have left detailed accounts of how Indian warriors scalped their foes. The first writer was a young French soldier, known to history by his initials, J.C.B. During the French and Indian War, J.C.B. spent several years in western Pennsylvania. He helped construct Fort DuQuesne, fought against Captain George Washington at Fort Necessity, and took part in the July 1755 battle along the Monongahela River, in which French soldiers and

Washington along the Monongahela in 1755

Indian warriors defeated an English army led by Major General Edward Braddock. In later years, J.C.B., writing in French, penned a lively memoir about his time in the military and gave much detail of his experiences in the Ohio River Valley. Titled *Travels in New France*, a 1941 English edition of his book contained a graphic description of how and why Indian warriors took the hair of people they captured, wounded, or killed during raids and battles.

A warrior, the Frenchman explained, used his tomahawk to hit the head of a prisoner or enemy. "When he has struck two or three blows, the savage quickly seizes his knife, and makes an incision around the hair from the upper part of the forehead to the back of the neck. Then he puts his foot on the shoulder of the victim, whom he has turned over face down, and pulls the hair off with both hands, from back to front ... This hasty operation is no sooner finished than the savage fastens the scalp to his belt and goes on his way."

J.C.B. reported that an Indian did this to a captive when he was being pursued or when the captive couldn't keep up as the warrior withdrew from the scene of the fighting. He took the prisoner's hair as "proof of his valor ... gives the death cry, and flees at top speed. Savages always announce their valor by a death cry, when they have taken a scalp. The English call it scalping."

The Frenchman elaborated:

When a savage has taken a scalp and is not afraid he is being pursued, he stops and scrapes the skin to remove the blood and fibers on it. He makes a hoop of green wood, stretches the skin over it like a tambourine, and puts it in the sun to dry a little. The skin is painted red, and the hair on the outside is combed. When prepared, the scalp is fastened to the end of a long stick, and carried on his shoulder in triumph to the village or place where he wants to put it. But as he nears each place on his way, he gives as many cries as he has scalps to announce his arrival and show his bravery. Sometimes, as many as 15 scalps are fastened on the same stick. When there are too many for one stick, they decorate several sticks with the scalps.

Bounties Offered

J.C.B. reported that the European officers offered bounties to Indians who came back from raids with scalps.

"The French ... were accustomed to pay for the scalps, to the amount of 30 francs' worth of trade goods," he said. "Their purpose was then to encourage the savages to take as many scalps as they could, and to know the number of the foe who had fallen. This precaution gave rise to a trick among the savages ... To increase the compensation received for scalps, they got the idea of making them of horsehide, which they prepared in the same way as human scalps. The discovery of this fraud was the reason they were more carefully inspected before a payment was made.

Consequently, the French and English finished by giving only a trifling amount in the form of presents."

The second description of scalping comes from a medical doctor named James Thacher, who served in the American Army during the Revolutionary War. In February 1776 he became a surgeon's mate in a regiment commanded by Colonel Asa Whitcomb that was stationed in Massachusetts. October 1777 found Thacher one of thirty surgeons and mates posted at a hospital near Albany, New York. "It is my lot to have 20 wounded men committed to my care," he wrote.

One of Thacher's patients was a Captain Greg, an officer in a New York regiment who had been stationed at a frontier post, Fort Stanwix, on the Mohawk River, near present-day Rome, N.Y.

Greg told the doctor that one day he and two of his soldiers had left the fort to shoot pigeons in a nearby woods. "A party of Indians started suddenly from concealment in the bushes, shot them all down, tomahawked and scalped them, and left them for dead."

As it turned out, the warriors had killed only two of the Americans. Although gravely wounded, the captain survived. At some point he regained consciousness. The war party was gone, but Greg's dog had stayed by his side. Greg sent the dog for help.

"The animal," Thacher wrote, "... ran about a mile when he met with two men fishing in the river." The dog managed to persuade the men to follow him back to his wounded master. The fishermen carried the captain to Fort Stanwix. "He was afterwards removed to our hospital and put under my care."

In his journal entry for October 24, 1777, Thacher recorded this sketch of the captain's wounds: "The whole of his scalp was removed. In two places in the forefront of his head, the tomahawk had penetrated through the skull. There was a wound on his back with the same instrument, beside a wound in his side and another through his arm by a musket ball."

Though condemned to a life without hair, the man eventually recovered, and the doctor described how his attacker had wounded him:

"The Indian mode of scalping is this: With a knife, they make a circular cut from the forehead, quite round, just above the ears, then taking hold of the skin with their teeth, they tear off the whole hairy scalp in an instant, with wonderful dexterity. This they carefully dry and preserve as a trophy, showing the number of their victims, and they have a method of painting on the dried scalp different figures and colors to designate the sex and age of the victim, and also the manner and circumstances of the murder."

A Captive's Story

During the 1750s, an immigrant named Thomas Jameson established a farmstead in a valley midway between present-day Gettysburg and Chambersburg. An Indian war party captured Jameson and most of his family in early April 1758. The war party killed and scalped Jameson, his wife, his older daughter, and two young sons. The Indians spared his fifteen-year-old daughter, Mary, but forced her to walk to across the Appalachian Mountains to Fort DuQuesne, a French fort at present-day Pittsburgh. Mary, who lived to be ninety, spent the rest of her life as an Indian. When a writer named James Seaver interviewed her in November 1823, she described how her captors forced her and two other prisoners to travel over the mountains. In the course of her narration, Mary Jemison offered this unflinching account of events that had happened along the trail one evening sixty-five years earlier:

'Hard Day's March'

After a hard day's march we encamped in a thicket, where the Indians made a shelter of boughs, and then built a good fire to warm and dry our benumbed limbs and clothing; for it had rained some through the day. Here we

Scalping a white woman

were again fed as before. When the Indians had
finished their supper, they took from their
baggage a number of scalps and went about
preparing them for the market, or to keep
without spoiling, by straining them over small
hoops which they prepared for that purpose,
and then drying and scraping them by the fire.
Having put the scalps, yet wet and bloody,
upon the hoops, and stretched them to their
full extent, they held them to the fire till they

were partly dried and then with their knives commenced scraping off the flesh; and in that way they continued to work, alternately drying and scraping them, till they were dry and clean. That being done, they combed the hair in the neatest manner, and then painted it and the edges of the scalps yet on the hoops, red.

Those scalps I knew at the time must have been taken from our family by the color of the hair. My mother's hair was red; and I could easily distinguish my father's and the children's from each other. That sight was most appalling; yet, I was obliged to endure it without complaining."

A week later, Mary accompanied the war party as it left Fort DuQuesne and sailed down the Ohio River in a large canoe. As the warriors set off, one man "took the scalps of my former friends (and) strung them on a pole that he placed upon his shoulder," she said later. These were trophies, and the war chief proudly displayed them as such.

'An Awful Spectacle'

"When the Indians relate their victories, they do not say they have taken so many 'scalps,' but so many 'heads,'" reported the Rev. John Heckewelder, a Moravian missionary who lived among the Delaware and Iroquois Indians for many years during the late eighteenth century. "They include ... those whom they have scalped, but left alive, which is sometimes the case, and their prisoners, as (well as) those whom they have killed."

"It is an awful spectacle to see the Indian warriors return home from a successful expedition with their prisoners and the scalps taken in battle. ... The scalps are carried in front, fixed on the end of a thin pole, about five or six feet in length; the prisoners follow, and the warriors advance shouting the dreadful scalp-yell ... For every head taken, dead or alive, a separate

John Heckewelder

shout is given. In this yell or whoop, there is a mixture of triumph and terror."

Heckewelder, who spoke the Delaware language, said, "the Indians pluck out all their hair except one tuft on the crown of their heads." They do this "to enable themselves to take off each other's scalps in war with greater facility." He said he had discussed this practice with Indians, who had explained:

"When we go to fight an enemy ... we meet on equal ground, and we take off each other's scalps, if we can. ... It would be ungenerous in a warrior to deprive an enemy of the means of acquiring that glory of which he himself is in pursuit."

The missionary once asked a friendly Indian why warriors just didn't let their hair grow.

"My friend," the man replied. "A human being has but one head, and one scalp from that head is sufficient to show that it has been in my power. Were we to preserve a whole head of hair, as the white people do, several scalps might be made of it, which would be unfair."

If Native Americans took the scalps of European settlers and soldiers—as well as those of other Indians —military records make it clear that Pennsylvania soldiers also scalped hostile Indians with some regularity during the French and Indian War. This happened even before the colony began paying bounties on Indian scalps. Pennsylvania offered the bounties as cash incentives to encourage white settlers to kill hostiles.

There's ample documentation that Pennsylvanians scalped hostile Indians. Consider an incident that occurred near Fort Hunter, a frontier post that farmers and other settlers hurriedly established in late 1755. Situated several miles north of modern Harrisburg, the post occupied a bluff overlooking the spot where Fishing Creek empties into the Susquehanna River's east side at present-day Rockville. It enjoyed a commanding view of the river, which, though shallow, is nearly a mile wide. In December 1755 soldiers caught an Indian above Fort Hunter. According to Conrad Weiser, a high-ranking officer, "The Indian begged his life and promised to tell all he knew. ... But they shot him ..., scalped him and threw his body in the river."

When Indians raided white settlements west of the Susquehanna in late 1755, a settler named James Patterson quickly organized a defensive force in the Juniata River Valley. He built a stockade fort at present-day Mexico in Juniata County, about forty miles northwest of present-day Harrisburg, and recruited twenty men to guard against Indian attacks. He believed that he could recruit more men if they could receive bounties for the scalps of any Indians that they killed.

Edward Shippen

Patterson asked Edward Shippen, a prominent Pennsylvanian who was instrumental in establishing a military force to protect the colony's western frontier, about this. In a December 16 letter, Shippen relayed Patterson's question on to William Allen, Pennsylvania's chief magistrate: "He wants very much to know whether any handsome premium is offered for scalps because, if there is, he is very sure his force will soon be augmented."

Cash for Scalps

At that time, Pennsylvania wasn't offering bounties for Indian scalps, but by April 1756, the colonial government started paying cash "for the scalps of enemy Indians." Government records from April 1756 show that by official proclamation, Pennsylvania offered $50 "for the scalp of every Indian woman" and $130 "for the scalp of every male Indian above 10 years old."

The prospect of collecting a bounty on Indian scalps clearly accelerated the practice. Consider an incident that occurred in the Upper Delaware River Valley in July 1756. A five-member patrol from Fort Hyndshaw, a frontier post along the Bushkill Creek near present-day Shawnee on the Delaware, had been sent to guard farmers about fifteen miles north of the fort. While doing this, the soldier encountered a party of three armed Indians. As Captain John Van Etten reported afterward, the sergeant engaged one of the Indians in a conversation, which seemed peaceable enough. But when the man suddenly attempted to run off, the soldiers fired at him, "killed him and took off his scalp."

These incidents may be construed as isolated acts of individual soldiers, but there's ample evidence that the scalping of Indians by whites quickly became a part of accepted military practices on the Pennsylvania frontier.

'Kill, Scalp, and Captivate'

In late 1756, for instance, Colonel William Clapham, the commandant at Fort Augusta, sent Captain John Hambright on a march up the Susquehanna River's West Branch at the head of a column consisting of two sergeants, two corporals, and thirty-eight privates. The colonel gave the captain explicit orders: "You are ... to attack, burn and destroy an Indian town on the West Branch of the Susquehanna. ... If any Indians are found there, you are to kill, scalp and captivate as many as you can ..."

Hambright's force left the fort on November 4. His scout was Andrew Montour, an Iroquois who was part French and who had once lived along the West Branch. Montour led the party fifty miles up the valley, past the present-day communities of Muncy, Montoursville, and Williamsport. He took them to a large, flat island that lies opposite the modern borough of Jersey Shore. Hambright's march ended without any Indians losing their hair—the natives had deserted the village before the soldiers got there.

Two Delaware warriors were so aggressive in attacking Pennsylvania settlements and forts that the provincial government put bounties on their heads. They were Shingas the Terrible and Captain Jacobs. In early April 1756 Delaware raiders swept into south-central Pennsylvania, overpowered Fort McCord, a private post northwest of present-day Chambersburg, then withdrew with an assortment of scalps and prisoners. A company of soldiers gave chase and followed the Indians more than forty miles into the mountains to the west. They joined forces with provincial soldiers who belonged to the garrison at Fort Lyttleton, and caught up with the Delawares at Sideling Hill. A spirited skirmish took place, and the Pennsylvanians were routed, with more than a score killed and nearly a dozen wounded. Shingas took part in the fighting, as did Captain Jacobs, and the retreating Pennsylvanians believed that one of their Indian allies, a Delaware named Isaac, had killed and scalped Captain Jacobs. A week later, Governor Morris instructed Elisha Saltar, who as commissary general of the provincial army was touring the colony's western forts, to "take upon oath what proofs you can of the certainty of Indian Isaac's having taken the scalp of Captain Jacobs, ... that Isaacs may be entitled to the reward."

As it turned out, Captain Jacobs had been neither killed nor scalped at Sideling Hill. Nearly four months later, he led Indians and French soldiers who captured and burned Fort Granville, a Pennsylvania post along

Andrew Montour

the Juniata River at present-day Lewistown. Five weeks after that, he was at home in his cabin in the Delaware town of Kittanning on the Allegheny River when a force of Pennsylvanians attacked the town at daybreak on September 8. The Indians resisted fiercely, but Jacobs was killed and scalped. The soldiers also liberated a number of white prisoners who had lived at Kittanning. In his official report of the raid, Lieutenant Colonel John Armstrong said that the "prisoners say they are perfectly assured of his scalp, as no other Indians there wore their hair in the same manner. They also say they know his squaw's scalp by a particular bob, and also know the scalp of a young Indian called the King's Son."

Satisfied that Captain Jacobs was dead, the Pennsylvania colonial government in late October awarded the colonel the sum of £272, a reward for both the Indian scalps and white prisoners he brought back from Kittanning.

A Widow's Request

As the French and Indian War progressed, individual whites living on the frontier came to regard the scalps of Indians for their cash value. Indeed, in 1757 Margaret Mitchell, a widow who lived in south-central Pennsylvania, requested payment for one. Writing from Shippensburg on October 25, Mrs. Mitchell complained to Richard Peters, an official of the Penn government in Philadelphia, that she was having difficulty in obtaining the bounty on a scalp that had somehow found its way into her possession. Some months earlier she had traveled to Philadelphia "in expectation of receiving a reward for an Indian scalp," even though she had been hard pressed "to take so fatiguing and expensive a journey." She had failed to find anyone willing to give her cash for the scalp and had returned home, still in possession of the scalp and still hopeful of receiving money for it. In her letter to Peters, Mrs. Mitchell explained that she had lost her husband and son in the war and that she needed the scalp bounty to pay for everyday living expenses. "One might think that common humanity might induce the gentlemen (colonial officials responsible for paying the scalp bounties) to allow some small matter," Mrs. Mitchell said.

Colonial documents that contained Margaret Mitchell's letter didn't indicate whether the woman ever received any cash for the scalp.

Disease Decimates Immigrants, Natives

Summer 1750

In 1750 a German musician named Gottfried Mittelberger traveled to Pennsylvania to be the organist and school teacher for the German congregation at St. Augustine's Church in Philadelphia. He was one of approximately four hundred passengers on a sailing ship that in early summer left the Netherlands, stopped for nine days at an English port, and then resumed its westward voyage to Philadelphia. Mittelberger didn't reach his destination until October 10; crossing the Atlantic had taken fifteen weeks.

The musician spent nearly four years in Philadelphia, then returned to Germany and wrote a book, *Journey to Pennsylvania*, in which he described his experiences at sea: "During the journey, the ship is full of pitiful signs of distress–smells, fumes, horrors, vomiting, various kinds of sea sickness, fever, dysentery, headaches, heat, constipation, boils, scurvy, cancer, mouth-rot, and similar afflictions, all of them caused by the age and the highly salted state of the food, especially the meat, as well as by the very bad and filthy water. ... There are so many lice, especially on the sick people, that they have to be scraped off the bodies."

"When waves and wind permitted, I held daily prayer meetings ... on deck, and, since we had no ordained clergyman on board, was forced to administer baptism to five children. I also held services, including a sermon, every Sunday, and, when the dead were buried at sea, commended them and our souls to the mercy of God."

Women and their newborn babies rarely survived childbirth at sea. "Children between the ages of one and seven seldom survive the sea voyage, and parents must often watch their offspring suffer miserably, die and be thrown in the ocean ... I myself, alas, saw such a pitiful fate overtake 32 children on board our vessel, all of whom were finally thrown into the sea. ... It is also worth noting that children who have not had either measles or smallpox usually get them on board the ship and for the most part perish as a result."

"The water distributed in these ships is often very black, thick with dirt, and full of worms. Even when very thirsty, one is almost unable to drink it ... To the end of our voyage, we had to eat the ship's biscuit, which had already been spoiled for a long time." The biscuits were often "full of red worms and spiders' nests."

"True, great hunger and thirst teach one to eat and drink everything—but many must forfeit their lives in the process."

Surviving a sea voyage was only one challenge for colonists on their way to North America. Blissfully unaware of the role of bacteria in spreading disease, European settlers brought primitive notions of cleanliness and sanitation to Pennsylvania. There's ample evidence that sickness killed more white settlers than hostile Native Americans ever did, and diseases inadvertently brought from the Old World devastated and decimated the Indians.

Peter Lindestrom spent several years on the Delaware River in the mid-1600s as a military engineer in the New Sweden Colony. He reported that the Mantessers, a band of Indians living along the river's east side in the vicinity of present-day Trenton, had been ravaged by warfare and disease. By 1654, these natives had mostly "died off," he said.

Smallpox Strikes
On the Susquehanna River, Dutch colonial officials reported in 1661 "a great mortality from smallpox

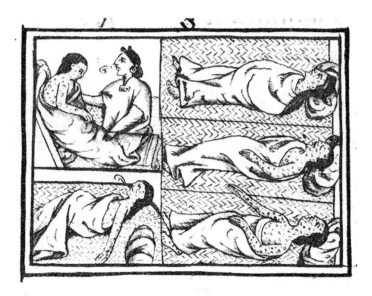

Smallpox killing the natives.

among the Minquas," Indians who were also known as the Susquehannocks.

In 1663 Swedish colonists recorded that "smallpox raged terribly among the Indians" along the lower Delaware and "ill-disposed people advised them to leap into the river and bathe themselves, whereby many perished."

A combination of sickness and warfare destroyed Indian communities along the lower Hudson River. Indeed, an English colonist named Daniel Denton reported that when the English had conquered New Amsterdam in 1664 and renamed the town New York, Indians in the vicinity were living in six towns. But by 1670, the year of Denton's report, "they are reduced to two small villages." Their reduction pleased Denton. "Where the English come to settle," he remarked, "a divine hand makes way for them by ... cutting off the Indians either by wars ... or by some raging mortal disease."

Natives succumbing to smallpox.

Wherever the Europeans settled in the Middle Atlantic colonies, diseases they unwittingly brought with them devastated native people who lived in the region. Consider the events that occurred along the New Jersey side of the Delaware River in the late 1670s. English colonists purchased land from the Indians, traded with them, and established the village of Burlington. Soon after, smallpox swept through native settlements and killed many. The settlers, who were Quakers, became fearful when they realized some Native Americans believed that the newcomers had deliberately exposed them to the disease. These Indians wanted to start a war against their new neighbors.

The Indian Kings

This happened "shortly after we came into the country," wrote Thomas Budd, one of the colonists. "Therefore we sent for the Indian kings to speak with them," Budd wrote in his 1685 book, *Good Order Established in Pennsylvania and New Jersey.* Accompanied by a large number of Indians, the chiefs

45

came to Burlington, where natives and colonists had a conference. "They were told," the chiefs said, "that we sold them the smallpox with the match coats they had bought of us." Although the conference proceeded peaceably, "the Indians told us they were advised to make war on us and cut us off whilst we were but few," Budd wrote.

The English denied that they had done anything to sicken the neighboring natives. They also pointed out that they had come "amongst them by their consent and had bought the land of them," Budd said. He noted that the settlers had paid for the land as well as for any "commodities we had bought at any time of them ..."

The chiefs accepted the remarks of the Burlington settlers. Budd quoted one as saying, "the smallpox ... was once in my grandfather's time, and it could not be the English that could send it to us then, there being no English in the country. And it was once in my father's time; they could not send it to us then neither. And now it is in my time. I do not believe that they have sent it to us now. I do believe it is the Man above that hath sent it ..."

The conference ended on a positive note. "We are minded to live in peace," the native speaker declared. "If we intend at any time to make war upon you, we will let you know of it and the reason why ... If you make us satisfaction for the injury done us, ... then we will not make war on you."

The Indians themselves knew that new diseases accompanied the Europeans. Along the Hudson River "we did not have so much sickness and death before the Christians came into the country," a native medicine man who had adopted the European nickname of Hans told Jaspar Dankers, a traveler from Holland, in 1680.

By the late 1600s, many Native Americans were convinced they were doomed if they continued to live among the Europeans. They "have a superstition that as many Indians must die each year as the number of

Europeans who newly arrive," reported Daniel Pastorius, a German immigrant who had settled near Philadelphia. Writing in 1683, Pastorius added that many natives wanted to withdraw from the European settlements in order to resettle "some hundred miles farther into the woods." Writing again in 1694, Pastorius, who was the founder of Germantown, remarked, "A great many of these savages have died since I came here" a decade earlier.

Graphic Account

The Moravian historian Loskiel gave a graphic account of how Indians reacted to the prospect of contracting a European disease. These Indians lived at Nain, a Moravian mission about a mile northwest of the village of Bethlehem. "The measles appearing at Nain in March 1759, the Indians were greatly alarmed. But when, out of 47 who were infected, not one died, those who had been timid and terrified for a while at the appearance of death were ashamed of their fears."

Notions of sanitation and disease were primitive among both Europeans and Native Americans. The daily life of Indians and colonists alike consisted of practices that contributed to the spread of disease.

Israel Acrelius, a Lutheran clergyman from Sweden, visited a sect of German Dunkards at a cloister at Ephrata in Lancaster County in August 1753. He described how the brethren sat down to the evening meal, which was served on a long table. The main courses—pumpkin mush and pearled barley boiled in milk—came to the table in deep stone dishes. After a prayer and reading of Scripture, "each one took out of his pocket a bag in which there was a wooden spoon and a knife. ... We all ate with a good appetite. ... When at the finishing of the dish, one could no longer use the spoon, the remainder was taken up with pieces of bread. ... At the close, each one licked his knife and spoon, dried them with a cloth which they had in the same bag, and then the knife and spoon were restored to their former place."

47

Cleanliness Uncommon

"Cleanliness is not common among the Indians," wrote George H. Loskiel, the eighteenth century historian. "Their pots, dishes and spoons are seldom washed, but left for the dogs to lick. The Delawares rather excel the Iroquois in cleanliness, and the Unami and Wawiachtano tribes are much cleaner than the Monseys. ... The dogs being continually in the house and at the fire, they bring fleas in abundance. Bugs and other vermin are numerous, but it is remarkable that the common fly resorts much more to the houses of the Europeans than to those of the Indians."

In writing his 1794 book, *History of the Mission of the United Brethren among the Indians of North America*, Loskiel drew upon diaries and letters of Moravian missionaries who had spent years living among the Indians in New York, Pennsylvania, Ohio, and other places.

Loskiel listed an assortment of diseases that afflicted Native Americans: "the pleurisy, weakness and pains in the stomach and breast, consumption, rheumatism, diarrhea, bloody flux, agues and inflammatory fevers. ... Floodings are common among the women, even in old age."

Indians dreaded the prospect of contracting smallpox. "They leave their nearest relations to die in the woods," Loskiel wrote. They "content themselves with bringing them a little food and drink." Indians sickened by smallpox "appear in despair and know not how to support life with patience. Most of them die before the smallpox appear."

When the French and Indian War came to eastern Pennsylvania, many Christian Indians took refuge in and around the Moravian community at Bethlehem. Late in 1756 "the smallpox broke out among the Indians, and it was so regulated that all those who were infected should retire beyond the Lecha (Lehigh River) where all possible care was taken of them," Loskiel reported.

Ship Captain's Ruse Foils Pirates

April 1654

February 1654: Bound for Swedish settlements along the lower Delaware River, a wooden sailing ship named *The Ohrn* departed Gothenburg, Sweden. Hundreds of happy passengers crowded her decks. They came mainly from farm families. To finance the crossing, they had sold their homesteads, livestock, and household furnishings. They were eager and excited to be under sail, bound for North America aboard a tall-masted vessel armed with cannon.

But as the voyage stretched into its seventh and eighth weeks, shipboard merriment dimmed, then subsided altogether. By the ninth week, Captain Johan Bockshorn realized *The Ohrn's* provisions wouldn't last to landfall. Moreover, "there were 230 and some persons sick," one of the passengers recorded. They suffered from an assortment of ills: fever, dysentery, ague, heartburn, "and it was impossible to hold out until New Sweden without refreshments," he wrote.

Heading South

So Captain Bockshorn turned *The Ohrn* south and headed for the Caribbean island of St. Christopher to buy supplies. Many passengers had died by the time the ship reached the island. "It could not have been otherwise," reported one passenger, a military engineer named Peter Lindestrom. "They were too closely packed together in the unnatural heat of the (April) sun. ... The common people had no clean linen for a change so that, speaking with respect, much vermin grew in their clothes. ... Besides, they had to content themselves with coarse and rotten victuals such as entirely decayed fish (and) putrid water ... in which grew long worms." Some mornings the people aboard *The Ohrn* awoke to learn that eight or nine passengers had died during the night.

On April 11 *The Ohrn* encountered three pirate ships that "pursued us hard," then closed in, Lindestrom wrote in *Geographia Americae*, his memoir of his experiences in New Sweden. A desperate Captain Bockshorn ordered all male passengers, sick and well alike, to go up to the deck. Passengers too ill to walk were carried to the deck "even if they were half-dead," Lindestrom said. Crew members quickly dispensed muskets, swords, clubs, spears, and other weapons to them. The captain ordered flasks of brandy passed among the passengers to strengthen their resolve. "Those who had not enough strength to stand were propped up and supported between two healthy men and so close together that the sick could lean on those who were well." The ruse succeeded. When the pirates saw the large number of armed men on the deck and counted the ship's cannon, they gave up pursuit.

Six weeks later, on May 20, *The Ohrn* sailed into the Delaware River and arrived in New Sweden. But after four months at sea, few passengers were joyous. "Most of them," wrote Lindestrom, "were sick or dead."

The arrival of a ship invariably attracted Indians from the surrounding areas. They had learned that ships brought not only provisions for the colonists but also trade goods that the Swedes bartered with the natives in exchange for furs, corn, and venison. If the arrival of *The Ohrn* created opportunities for Indians and Swedes to trade, it also allowed the Indians to be exposed to diseases brought ashore by the sick travelers. Within a month of the ship's arrival, sickness swept through the native settlements and killed a substantial number of Indians. Chiefs who survived were infuriated. On prior occasions, they had recognized that their villages were subject to outbreaks of disease in the weeks following the arrival of a ship from Sweden.

Ten Chiefs

This became a key issue on June 17, when ten chieftains met with the whites at Printz Hall on Tinicum Island, a large island in the Delaware just below present-day Philadelphia. The chiefs included Quirocus and Peminacka from Passyunk and Naaman from along the Delaware in Bucks County. As Israel Acrelius, a Swedish clergyman, recounted in his 1759 history of New Sweden, "The Indians complained that our ships had brought much evil upon them, as so many of them had since died," the Swedes recorded. But the Swedes denied that their ships had imported evil spirits especially to kill off the Indians. "Many of our own people were dying" also, they said.

Even so, one chief (surviving accounts of the meeting fail to identify him) rejected the Europeans' contention. He insisted that an evil spirit—a "Bad Manitho"—had accompanied *The Ohrn* to New Sweden and that, unless it was driven away, "all would die," Indians and Swedes alike. This chief declared that he and other Indians had seen evidence of this spirit in the water, sparkling "like fire all around the ship."

This notion struck the Swedes as ridiculous. "We told them it was nothing else but the salt water which ... sparkled and which had ... sparkled thus throughout our whole voyage," they said in reply. Their rebuttal angered the sachem, and he spoke directly to the colonist who had made the remark. "You are crazy, you old fool," the Indian exclaimed heatedly. "Have I and some others not seen that?"

At this point, the Swedish interpreter, speaking tactfully and kindly, managed to mollify the chiefs and distributed gifts to them. This defused the tension, and the Lenape chief called Namaan reproached his colleagues for their anger. In his history, Acrelius quoted Namaan as saying that the Swedes "were good people." "Waving his hands around as if he were tying

51

a tight knot," the sachem vowed that as a gourd "is a round growth without a rent or seam, so should we (Indians and Swedes) hereafter be as one head without a crack."

Indians Herd Horses, Cattle across Pennsylvania

Summer 1772

The summer of 1772 presented hardships and challenges for the Moravian missionaries and the 240 Native Americans living at Wyalusing on the Susquehanna River's North Branch.

Known as Friedenshutten, the seven-year-old mission had a chapel, school house, fifty-two log houses constructed mainly of squared white pine timbers, and assorted huts and outbuildings. But the Indian congregation, feeling pressed by expansionist-minded Pennsylvanians, had decided to move west—to Ohio, even though this meant abandoning their well-cultivated farmlands, neat gardens enclosed by fences, and fruit trees.

It was June 11 when the Indians and the missionaries struck out for the west. They included children, adults, healthy people, and even invalids, including a crippled child whose mother carried him on her back.

The caravan moved out despite rain that had lasted for days. Some of the emigrants walked along an overland trail that led to modern Montoursville, some fifty miles to the west. They took the livestock— mostly horses and a herd of horned cows—they had raised at Friedenshutten.

Others sailed downriver in dugout canoes that also carried provisions and the heavy tools the Indians would need to build new mission towns in Ohio: "plow irons, harrow teeth, pick axes, all kinds of farming utensils and tools, iron pots and large brass kettles for the boiling of maple sugar," according to the Rev. John

Heckewelder, who in 1820 published a history of the Moravian mission to the Indians.

The fleet rounded the point at the new town of Northumberland, then paddled up the West Branch and met the overland travelers on June 20, not far from present-day Muncy.

The overland trek proved difficult. The route lay through dense forests, and "the path was frequently a blind one, and yet along it 60 head of cattle and 50 horses and colts had to be driven, and it needed careful watch to keep them together," missionary John Ettwein wrote in his diary.

Wandering Off

When the travelers camped for the night, a cow or horse invariably wandered off. Each morning the Indians went looking for missing livestock.

"At our first night's encampment, two of our Indians lost themselves while in search of straying cattle, and several hours elapsed before we could reach them with signal guns," Ettwein wrote.

The missionary was impressed by the high quality of the land that lay between the North and West Branches. "There were exceedingly rich bottoms and the noblest timber I have seen in America, excepting the cypress in South Carolina and Georgia," Ettwein noted.

The travelers came upon the headwaters of Muncy Creek then followed the trail as it descended to the West Branch. "It rained incessantly, and I was wet all day," Ettwein wrote. "The path led 36 times across Muncy Creek."

June 14 was Trinity Sunday, and Ettwein attempted to hold a worship service in the woods, "but the incessant lowing and noise of the cattle drowned all attempts at discourse and singing," he said.

On June 15 Ettwein's group passed "into an extensive and beautiful region of plains. Here the hunters in two days shot 15 deer, the meat of which was dried at the fires for use on the journey."

John Ettwein

The frontier lacked any kind of organized postal service, and Ettwein was pleased when, on Friday, June 17, the emigrants met a traveler from New Jersey, "who on his way home would pass through Bethlehem," the base of the Moravian Church. Quick to spot an opportunity, Ettwein "handed him letters for home."

The next day, a Saturday, they camped near Samuel Wallis's farm between present-day Muncy and

Montoursville. Clergymen rarely visited the valley, and the settlers eagerly invited Ettwein to hold services on Sunday, June 21.

He did. "At noon I preached to from 50 to 60 hearers, all English, some of whom had come a distance of 20 miles," Ettwein said.

On Monday "We had a market day in camp," the missionary reported. "Mr. Wallis bought ... 15 head of young cattle and some canoes. Others [purchased] bowls, [small, wooden containers called] firkins, buckets, tubs and diverse iron ware."

The Indian travelers were Christians who didn't drink alcoholic beverages. Even so, "a trader's agent smuggled some rum into the ... camp," Ettwein recorded. "When discovered, we handed the contraband to Mr. Wallis for safe-keeping until the trader should return."

Emigrating as a congregation—some in canoes, others on foot—the travelers encountered gnats, snakes, and sickness along the way. They reached present-day Jersey Shore on June 25, camping along the West Branch, across from a large island.

Rattlesnakes Plentiful

"Here the rattlesnakes seemed to hold an undisputed sway, and they were killed at all points," Ettwein wrote in his journal. "A horse was brought in that had been bitten in the nose. His head swelled up frightfully ... and the poor animal perished the next day."

As leader of the expedition, Ettwein grew increasingly concerned that his parishioners would run out of food if they didn't make better time. "Today," he wrote on June 26, "I assembled the men, told them that we had progressed but 30 miles during the past week and that if we failed to make more rapid headway, our large company would come to want."

June 27 found them near present-day Lock Haven, "where we met Mr. Anderson, who dissuaded us from attempting to embark in canoes, stating that the water was too shallow." So the emigrants sold the canoes to the settlers living in the region, and began carrying overland the farm implements and other heavy materials they had shipped this far by canoe.

On June 29 Ettwein marked his fifty-second birthday. On the thirtieth "I trod upon a 15-year-old rattlesnake." His Indian companions killed the reptile, and Ettwein wasn't harmed. Nonetheless, "for days, I took every step with dread, fancying every rustling leaf to be the movement of a venomous serpent."

There were other dangers as well. Crossing a rocky, swift stream on July 8, "I fell neck deep into the water," the missionary noted.

The caravan included children, adults, and several invalids. Several children came down with measles. One of them was "a poor little cripple, aged 10 years ... whom his mother had carried all the way in a basket," Ettwein said. His name was Nathan.

On July 11, Nathan died. "His emaciated remains were interred along the side of the path, and I cut his name into a tree that overshadowed his lonely grave," Ettwein wrote.

Then the travelers moved on. They came to Chinklacamoose (present-day Clearfield) on Thursday, July 16.

"We found but three huts and a few patches of Indian corn," Ettwein wrote. "The name signifies, 'No one tarries here willingly.'"

The Moravian congregation certainly didn't. The next day, somewhere west of Clearfield, the trail left the West Branch and headed overland. "The path went precipitately up the mountains to the summit to a spring, the first waters of the Ohio," the missionary wrote.

Place of Gnats

By July 19 the travelers reached Punxsutawney, camped in the rain, and encountered gnats—*ponkis* in the Indian language—with a nasty bite.

"In the evening," Ettwein said, "the *ponkis* were excessively annoying, so that the cattle pressed … into our camp to escape their persecutors in the smoke of the fires. This vermin is a plague to man and beast, both by day and night."

At this place insects were so plentiful, "the Indians call it *Ponks-utenink*—the Town of the *Ponkis*. The word is equivalent to 'living dust and ashes,'" he said.

The Indians told Ettwein that thirty years earlier a native sorcerer had often robbed and murdered other Indians here. One day a warrior killed the sorcerer and "burned his bones. The wind blew his ashes into the swamp and they became living things, and hence the *ponkis*," Ettwein wrote.

Notwithstanding gnats, snakes, and inclement weather, the Moravians pressed on. It was August 23 when the missionaries and Indians finally reached the Tuscarawas River in Ohio. The trek had taken them two months and two weeks.

Native Americans Wrote on Trees

Summer 1775

The summer of 1775 a missionary named Philip Vickers Fithian rode his horse far into the Pennsylvania frontier. The young Presbyterian clergyman traveled up the Susquehanna River's West Branch, where he preached to European settlers that he encountered along the way. Fithian wrote in his journal that he had reached present-day Lock Haven (about 165 miles above Harrisburg) in late July. The morning of Sunday, July 30, "I began service at 11 ... on the bank of the river, opposite to the Great Island. ... There were present about a hundred and forty. I stood at the root of a great tree and the people sitting in the bush and on the green grass around me. They gave great attention. I had the eyes of all upon me. I spoke with some force and pretty loud. ..."

The next morning, accompanied by a man named Gilaspee, Fithian struck out for what has become south-central Pennsylvania. Guide and missionary took an overland course intended to take them across the mountains separating the Susquehanna's West Branch and the Juniata River far to the south. The trail took them through a virgin forest with tall trees that had thick trunks. "We rode through a wild wilderness twenty miles up Bald Eagle Creek without the sight of a single house. We saw many Indian camps, small crotched sticks covered with thick bark. ... On the bank of a brook which ran into the creek, at length, we came to a fire. Some Indians or others had camped there last night. Near the fire and over the very road hung half a deer. The two hind quarters ... were yet warm. Mr. Gilaspee alighted and wrapped

Charcoal drawing of Philip Vickers Fithian, Princeton Class of 1772, by an unknown artist.

them with some green bushes in his surtout," which was a long overcoat.

Around midday, Fithian and Gilaspee came to the house of Andrew Bogg, and "we dined on fish ... and on venison." When they had finished the meal, "Gilaspee threw himself on a blanket and is now asleep," the missionary wrote. As for Fithian, "I sat me down on a three-legged stool, to writing."

He recorded his impressions of the morning's ride up the Bald Eagle Creek, and reported: "Many of the trees on this road are cut by the Indians in strange figures; in diamonds—death's heads—crowned heads —initial letters—whole names—dates of years— blazes."

The missionary had encountered an instance of Native American picture writing. The journals kept by Fithian and other educated travelers make it clear that Indians regularly drew maps, pictures, and symbols to make records of their personal exploits. As they journeyed through the forests and along the rivers, they left information along the trail for other travelers.

During the summer of 1755, for instance, pro-French warriors had been harassing a British army led by Major General Edward Braddock as it marched across western Pennsylvania. Ever so slowly, Braddock's force had made its way west and north from Virginia, coming by way of Winchester and across present-day Maryland, past Fort Cumberland on the Wills Creek, and eventually reaching the Youghiogeny River in late June.

On June 24 the officers had the men up and marching by five in the morning. "In the day's march," reported Captain Orme, "we discovered an Indian camp, which they had just abandoned. ... They had stripped and painted some trees, upon which they and the French had written many threats and bravados ..." The paintings added to the discomfort of Braddock's men, who were already uncomfortable just from being in the desolate, heavily forested country.

The soldiers advanced about six miles that day then camped. At daybreak the next morning, three men went out beyond the sentinels, presumably looking for horses that had strayed during the night. Lurking Indians shot and scalped them then fled.

The British pressed on, passed the Great Meadows where the Virginians had built Fort Necessity the year before, and kept a watchful eye for French and Indians. At one point, the captain reported the advanced sentinels fired on Indians and French attempting to reconnoiter the camp.

Hampered by poor roads, the expedition progressed only four miles on June 26. "At our halting place," Orme said, "we found another Indian camp which they had abandoned at our approach, their fires being yet burning. They had marked in triumph upon trees the scalps they had taken two days before, and a great many French had also written their names and many insolent expressions."

The officer said, "The Indian camp was in a strong position, being upon a high rock with a very narrow and steep ascent to the top. It had a spring in the middle, and stood at the termination of the Indian path to the Monongahela, at the confluence of Redstone Creek."

A System of Glyphs

The Rev. John Heckewelder, a Moravian missionary who spent decades living among the Delaware Indians during the late 1700s, reported that, especially when traveling, Indians used their system of writing to convey information to other travelers. "For instance, on a piece of bark or on a large tree with the bark taken off for the purpose, by the side of a path, they can and do give every necessary information to those who come the same way."

Heckewelder wrote a detailed account of how this worked: If the Indians belong to a war party, they will report that they were a war party of so many men from such a place, of such a nation and such a tribe; how many men of each tribe were in the party; to which tribe the chief or captain belonged; in what direction they proceeded to meet the enemy; how many days they were out and how many returning; what number of the enemy they had killed; how many prisoners they had brought; how many scalps they had taken; whether they had lost any of their party, and how many; what enemies they had met with, and how many they had consisted of; of what nation or tribe their captain was, etc., all of which at a single glance is perfectly well understood by them. In the same manner they describe a chase.

The missionary's account, which appears in his book, *History, Manners and Customs of the Indian Nations Who Once Inhabited Pennsylvania and the Neighboring States*, said this practice was widespread: "All Indian nations can do this although they have not all the same marks; yet I have seen the Delawares read with ease the drawings of the Chippeways, Mingoes, Shawanos and Wyandots on similar subjects."

Examples of Native American writing are plentiful. They include the accounts detailed below.

Drawing Maps

The summer of 1750, two Moravian travelers—David Zeisberger and Bishop John Frederick Cammerhoff—were traveling along Cayuga Lake in western New York. Their guide, whom Cammerhoff often refers to as "our Gajuka," was named Hahotschaunquas. A second Indian also accompanied them.

They were in the vicinity of modern Ithaca, NY and had stopped for the night.

We had a long conversation with the Gajuka (Cayuga) and the other Indian concerning the lakes in this neighborhood. The Gajuka, who has traveled much through this region, drew a map on a piece of dry bark and showed how one could go by water from Gajuka into the St. Lawrence and in like manner to Niagara Falls. He also told us that the Susquehanna did not rise from the lakes, but that it gradually grew very small and almost disappeared, and that soon after branches from small lakes, of which they pointed out several, flowed into it and formed it. We conversed until late and went to bed in a comfortable frame of mind.

JOHN L. MOORE

In late June or early July 1755, a young Pennsylvanian named James Smith was imprisoned at Fort DuQuesne, a French post at the confluence of the Allegheny and Monongahela Rivers. A Delaware Indian who had belonged to the war party that had captured Smith some weeks earlier near present-day Bedford visited him in the fort. Smith reported that the man "spoke ... bad English, ... I found him to be a man of considerable understanding. ... I asked him what news from Braddock's army? ... He showed me by making marks on the ground with a stick that Braddock's army was advancing in very close order and that the Indians would surround them, take trees, and, as he expressed it, 'Shoot um down, all one pigeon.'"

In 1758 Colonel Henry Bouquet led an English army west from Carlisle to dislodge the French at Fort DuQuesne. Writing to General John Forbes, his superior officer, from Fort Loudoun on June 16, 1758, Bouquet reported that he had met a force of ninety-nine Cherokees and twenty-seven Catawba Indians at the fort. They had come north from the southern colonies to take part in the campaign against Fort DuQuesne. Although the Cherokees had intended to return to the South, they had "after two days of intrigue, dinners and public counsels ... resolved to follow us everywhere you may want to lead us," Bouquet wrote.

The Cherokees insisted that they knew the Ohio territory. Bouquet reported: "One of the chiefs told me that they were acquainted with the country where we were going, and so that I would have no doubt of it, he made a sign to one of his warriors who has lately returned from Fort DuQuesne to sketch his march. He took his knife and drew a map on the table from Winchester (in Virginia) to Fort DuQuesne, with all the rivers and roads which lead there, entering into the smallest details on the nature of the ground, which is said to be mountainous everywhere except along the Monongahela, but it is passable almost the whole way."

War Records

On Tuesday, June 5-16, 1750, Zeisberger and Cammerhoff, the Moravians traveling in New York, happened upon a grove of trees that the Cayuga Indians used as a library.

We reached a creek called by the Indians Gientachne, where their warriors usually encamped. Here we saw the whole chancery court or archives of the Gajukas, painted or hanging in the trees. Our Gajuka gave us a lengthy explanation of it all. When the great warriors go to war against the Gatabes (Catawba Indians), they make a painting of themselves. We saw several of these fine works of art, done in Indian-style. On their return, they add their deeds in a painting, showing what scalps they have taken, what they bring with them in the shape of treasures, bracelets, wampum and the like.

The Gajuka pointed out to us, with much importance, what he had himself painted as he had been to war twice. The one time he had brought back eight prisoners and two scalps, and on the other occasion three prisoners.

In June 1763, a Quaker preacher, John Woolman, traveled along the Lehigh Path in northeastern Pennsylvania as he headed for the Susquehanna River's North Branch. Woolman had left Philadelphia, stopped one night at the Moravian community of Bethlehem, then traveled along the Lehigh River toward Fort Allen, a military post that Ben Franklin had built nearly a decade earlier at present-day Weissport. Woolman had several Indian guides, and headed north toward the Wyoming Valley.

Woolman's party crossed the Lehigh near the fort on June 10. "The water being high, we went over in a canoe," he wrote. "After traveling some miles, we met several Indian men and women with a cow and horse, and some household goods, who were lately come from

David Zeisberger

their dwelling at Wyoming, and were going to settle at another place. We made them some small presents. ...

"We pitched our tent near the banks of the same river, having labored hard in crossing some of those mountains called the Blue Ridge," he continued to write.

As he explored the campsite, Woolman was surprised to find paintings that Indian artists had made in the forest and described them in the following: "Near our tent, on the sides of large trees peeled for that purpose, were various representations of men going to and returning from the wars, and of some being killed in battle. This being a path heretofore used by warriors, and ... I walked about viewing those Indian histories, which were painted mostly in red but some in black."

Woolman noted that it was the tenth of June —"Tenth of sixth month," according to the Quaker convention.

Travel Notes

In July 1750 the Moravian travelers Zeisberger and Cammerhoff had left Onondaga and were headed back to Pennsylvania. "We started early and were obliged to climb a very high mountain," Cammerhoff wrote on Saturday, July 14-25, 1750. "We went on till in the evening we reached the War Camp. By the paintings on the trees, we at once discovered that our Gajuka had been there. He had shot three bears and three deer and had slept here for three nights. All this we could tell from the horses and figures painted on the trees. We spent a comfortable night here."

In April 1780 a Pennsylvanian named Thomas Peart and fourteen others were taken prisoners during a raid that Captain Rowland Montour led on settlements north of present-day Allentown along the Mahoning Creek, a tributary of the Lehigh River.

Peart, who survived the ordeal, subsequently reported that his captors took him and two other prisoners to western New York. For several days the war party had been hiking along the Cayuga Creek. His group had gone ahead of some other Indians and camped for two nights in the expectation that the others would join them, but by morning of the third day "they became impatient of waiting for the others" and resumed the journey. "After traveling till near noon, they made a short stay, stripping the bark off a tree, and then painted, in their Indian manner, themselves and the prisoners on the body of the tree. This done, they set up a stick with a slit at the top, in which they placed a small bush of leaves, and leaned the stick so that the shadow of the leaves should fall to the point where it was fixed in the ground, by which means, the others would be directed in the time of day when they left the place."

In short, the warriors had fashioned a rustic sort of sun dial to supplement the data they had left upon the trees.

Indian Hunters Often Used Fire as Weapon

December 1632

David DeVries, an early Dutch navigator, said that as he sailed along the Atlantic seacoast, he could sometimes smell America before he saw it. That was because the natives had set the woods afire, and the winds blew the smoke out over the sea.

A trader as well as a navigator, De Vries made four voyages to the Americas between 1620 and 1644. In early December 1632 he was sailing north from St. Martin in the West Indies, hugging the coast along Virginia and Maryland to the north of the Chesapeake Bay. He was headed for the New Netherlands Colony and, more specifically, a spot near present-day Lewes, Delaware, where in 1631 he had established a plantation that was both a whaling station and trading post. De Vries wrote in his journal that the night of December 1, he anchored in fourteen fathoms (about eighty-four feet) of water "and smelt the land, which gave a sweet perfume as the wind came from the northwest. ... This comes from the Indians setting fire at this time of year to the woods and thickets in order to hunt, and the land is full of sweet smelling herbs as sassafras ... When the wind blows out of the northwest and the smoke is driven to sea, the land is smelt before it is seen."

De Vries was one of at least four European writers who came to North America prior to 1655 and reported that Indians living in what became the New Netherlands and the Virginia colonies routinely set fire to the forests to facilitate their hunts or to clear the ground for the cultivation of crops such as corn. Some of these writers also told about Indians going out in

David deVries

large and highly organized groups to hunt for deer and other animals.

Indeed, Captain John Smith reported in a book printed in England in 1612 that Indians living in Virginia occupied villages located among corn fields. Individual houses were often separated "by groves of trees," Smith wrote. "Near their habitations is little small wood, or old trees on the ground, by reason of their burning of them for fire so that a man may gallop a horse amongst these woods any way, but where the creeks or rivers shall hinder."

Hundreds of miles to the north in present-day New York, Native Americans also employed fire. "The Indians have a yearly custom of burning the woods, plains and meadows in the fall of the year when the leaves have fallen and when the grass and vegetable substances are dry," wrote Adriaen Van der Donck, a Dutch lawyer who emigrated to New Netherlands in 1641.

One reason Indian men did this was "to render hunting easier, as the brush and vegetable growth renders the walking difficult for the hunter, and the crackling of the dry substances betrays him and frightens away the game," Van der Donck said.

Another reason: "To circumscribe and enclose the game within the lines of the fire, when it is more easily taken, and also because the game is more easily tracked over the burned parts of the woods."

'Bush Burning'

This practice, which Van der Donck said was called "bush burning," had a beneficial effect on the forest since it would "thin out and clear the woods of all dead substances and grass, which grow better the ensuing spring."

As fire progressed through the forest, "it frequently spreads and rages with such violence that it is awful to behold," the colonist wrote. Nonetheless, "the green trees do not suffer. The outside bark is scorched three or four feet high, which does them no injury." He described instances, however, where fire "in thick pine woods" consumed dead trees that had toppled over. Flames spread to the tree tops and "the entire tops of trees are sometimes burnt off. ... Frequently great injuries are done by such fires, but the burning down of entire woods never happens," he said.

Van der Donck arrived in the Colony of Rensselaerwyck, a settlement on the upper Hudson River near present-day Albany, in August 1641 and spent several years there. Indians who lived in the vicinity often employed this technique of forest management, reported Van der Donck, who lived along the upper Hudson for five years before moving to what is known now as the Bronx in 1646

"I have seen many instances of wood-burning in the Colony of Rensselaerwyck, where there is much pine wood," he wrote. "Those fires appear grand at night from the passing vessels in the river when the woods are burning on both sides ... Then we can see a great distance by the light of the blazing trees, the flames being driven by the wind and fed by the tops of the trees. But the dead and dying trees remain burning in their standing positions, which appear sublime and beautiful when seen at a distance."

Colonists reported seeing similar hunting techniques used by Indians along the Delaware River. For instance, Peter Lindestrom, a Swedish military engineer who arrived in New Sweden in 1654, reported that by late winter, "the grass ... is as dry as hay." The Indian hunters form a circle several miles in diameter. They uproot enough grass to fashion a fire wall wide enough to prevent the flames from burning the wrong way. Then they torch the grass "so that the fire travels away in towards the center of the circle. ... The Indians follow with great noise, and all the animals that are found within the circle flee from the fire." All this time, the circle of fire becomes smaller and smaller, and the animals are driven toward the center.

As the circle becomes increasingly smaller, the hunters eventually stop "so that they mutually cannot do each other any harm. Then they break loose with guns and arrows on the animals." Trapped, the animals cannot escape, and the Indians "get a great multitude of all kinds of animals which are found there."

Lindestrom also reported that following the first hunt of the year, Indians living along the Delaware River arranged a community celebration and feasted on the animals they had killed. Whatever remained of

Captain John Smith

the carcasses when the Indians had finished eating became what Lindestrom called "a burnt offering ... to Manitto." After that, "they sing and dance and when they become jolly and happy, then they cry and sing ... 'Hagginj (pronounced "hah-gin-ni"), ha, ha, ha. Hagginj ha. Hagginj ha. Hagginj ha. Hagginj ha, ha, ha.'"

'Many Fires'

Captain John Smith reported in his 1612 book, *A Map of Virginia. With a Description of the Countrey*," that organized groups of Indian hunters used fire when pursuing deer. "Having found the deer," Smith wrote, "they environ (surround) them with many fires, and betwixt the fires they place themselves. And some take their stands in the midst. The deer being thus feared by the fires and their voices, they chase them so long within that circle, that many times they kill six, eight, 10, or 15 at a hunting."

Organized Hunting

The Indians of Virginia also used a form of organized hunting that didn't depend on fire. "They ... also ... drive them into some narrow point of land, when they find that advantage; and so force them into the river, where with their boats they have ambuscadoes to kill them," Smith said. "When they have shot a deer by land, they follow him like blood hounds by the blood and strain, and oftentimes so take them. Hares, partridges, turkeys, or eggs, fat or lean, young or old, they devour all they can catch ..."

Samuel de Champlain, writing about his 1615 voyage to New France, described the group hunting techniques that Canadian Indians used. The explorer had accompanied a large number of native hunters armed with bows, arrows, and spears along a river that emptied into Lake Ontario's northern shore. Hunters carrying bows went into the forest, while others equipped with spears stayed in canoes at pre-arranged spots along the river. "They place four or five hundred savages in line in the woods so that they extend to certain points on the river, then marching in order ... shouting and making a great noise in order to frighten the beasts, they continue to advance until the come to the end of the point. Then all the animals between the point and the hunters are forced to throw themselves into the water."

Animals that seek escape in the river are quickly hunted down by Indians in canoes who "easily approach the stags and other animals, tired out and greatly frightened in the chase." Invariably, some of

Samuel de Champlain

the animals caught up in the drive don't run into the river, and instead remain on the land. These "fall by the arrows shot at them by the hunters," Champlain said.

Champlain described another style of group hunting that he observed in November 1615. This hunt took place along a stream in what is now the Province of Ontario. A team of some twenty-five Indians spent ten days in erecting a triangle-shaped enclosure, which the explorer described as closed on two sides and open on the third. The two sides were 1,500 paces long and were "made of great stakes of wood closely pressed together, from eight to nine feet high," he wrote. Where these two sides came together, the hunters made what he called "a little enclosure, constantly diminishing in size, covered in part with boughs and with only an opening of five feet, about the width of a medium-sized door into which the deer were to enter."

As the day of the hunt approached, other Indians arrived to take part. About half an hour before daybreak, they split into two groups, "separated from each other (by) some 80 paces," Champlain said. Each Indian "had two sticks, which they struck together, and they marched in this order at a slow pace until they arrived at the enclosure." Frightened by the noise and the movement, the deer moved toward the wall of stakes. When the animals reached the triangle, the hunters began shooting arrows at them, and this forced the surviving deer farther into the enclosure. Then the hunters use a new tactic. "On reaching the end of the triangle, they begin to shout and imitate wolves ... The deer, hearing this frightful noise, are constrained to enter the retreat by the little opening, whither they are very hotly pursued by arrow shots." This pen is "so well closed and fastened that they can by no possibility get out (and) they are easily captured."

Champlain reported that he and the Indians remained at this camp for thirty-eight days, with the natives staging hunts of this type every other day. During this time, "they captured one hundred and twenty deer," he said. This works out to about six deer per hunt.

Native Tool Makers Fashioned Heart-Shaped Arrow Heads

Captain John Smith left a highly detailed account of how Indian hunters that he saw in Virginia made and used their weapons:

> For fishing and hunting and wars, they use much their bow and arrows. They bring their bows to the form of ours by the scraping of a shell. Their arrows are made, some of straight young sprigs, which they head with bone some

two or three inches long. These they use to shoot at squirrels on trees.

Another sort of arrows they use, made of reeds. These are pieced with wood, headed with splinters of crystal or some sharp stone, the spurs of a turkey, or the bill of some bird.

For his knife, he hath the splinter of a reed to cut his feathers in form. With this knife also, he will joint a deer or any beast; shape his shoes, buskins, mantels, &c.

To make the notch of his arrow he hath the tooth of a beaver set in a stick, wherewith he grateth it by degrees. His arrowhead he quickly maketh with a little bone, which he ever weareth at his bracer, of any splint of a stone, or glass in the form of a heart; and these they glue to the end of their arrows. With the sinews of deer, and the tops of deer horns boiled to a jelly, they make a glue that will not dissolve in cold water.

Bow Hunting

Bows and arrows were also important in catching fish. Smith reported:

Their fishing is much in boats. These they make of one tree by burning and scratching away the coals with stones and shells till they have made it in form of a trough. Some of them are an elne (42 or 45 inches) deep, and 40 or 50 foot in length, and some will bear 40 men; but the most ordinary are smaller, and will bear 10, 20, or 30, according to their bigness. Instead of oars, they use paddles and sticks, with which they will row faster than our barges.

Betwixt their hands and thighs, their women ... spin the barks of trees, deer sinews, or a kind of grass they call pemmenaw; of these they make a thread very even and readily. This thread serveth for many uses, as about their housing, apparel; as also they make nets for fishing, for the quantity as formally braided as ours. They also make with it lines for angles (fishing).

Their hooks are either a bone grated, as they nock their arrows, in the form of a crooked pin or fishhook; or of the splinter of a bone tied to the cleft of a little stick, and with the end of the line, they tie on the bate.

They use also long arrows tied in a line wherewith they shoot at fish in the rivers. But they of Accawmack use staves like unto javelins headed with a bone. With these they dart fish swimming in the water.

Selected Bibliography

Booth, Russell H. Jr. *The Tuscarawas Valley in Indian Days 1750-1797* Cambridge, Ohio: Gomber House Press, 1995.

Bouquet, Henry. *The Papers of Henry Bouquet*, Volume II: The Forbes Expedition. Edited by S. K. Stevens, Donald H. Kent and Autumn L. Leonard. Harrisburg, PA: the Pennsylvania Historical and Museum Commission, 1951.

The Colonial Image. Edited by John C. Miller. New York: George Braziller, Inc.,1962.

Colonial Records. vol. VII. Harrisburg, PA: Theo. Fenn & Co., 1851.

Heckewelder, John Gottlieb Ernestus. *An Account of the History, Manners, and Customs of the Indian Nations, Who Once Inhabited Pennsylvania and the Neighboring States.* Philadelphia: Publication Fund of the Historical Society of Pennsylvania, 1876. (Reprint edition by Arno Press Inc., 1971)

Hunter, William A. *Forts of the Pennsylvania Frontier, 1753-1758.* Harrisburg: Pennsylvania Historical and Museum Commission, 1960.

Loudon, Archibald. *A Selection of Some of the Most Interesting Narratives of Outrages Committed by the Indians in Their Wars with the White People.* 1808-1811, vols. I and II. Carlisle, PA: The Press of A. Loudon, 1811. (Reprint edition by Garland Publishing Inc., 1977.)

Pennsylvania Archives. First Series. vols. I and II. Edited by Samuel Hazard. Philadelphia: Joseph Severns & Co., 1853.

Seaver, James. *A Narrative of the Life of Mrs. Mary*

Jemison. Canandaigua, NY: J. D. Beamis and Co., 1824. (Reprint edition by Garland Publishing Inc., New York, 1977.)

Swift, Robert B. *The Mid-Appalachian Frontier: A Guide to Historic Sites of the French and Indian War.* Gettysburg, PA: Thomas Publications, 2001.

Wallace, Paul A. W. *Indian Paths of Pennsylvania.* Harrisburg: Pennsylvania Historical and Museum Commission, 1971.

Zeisberger, David. *David Zeisberger's History of North American Indians.* Edited by Archer Butler Hulbert and William Nathaniel Schwarze. Columbus, Ohio: Press of F. J. Heer, 1910.

95178651R00052

Made in the USA
Columbia, SC
13 May 2018